HERE ARE THE CUSTOMERS' YACHTS

How to Systematically Buy Low, Sell High, and Earn Lifetime Profits

By

Jeffrey Weber

Copyright and Use Notice

Disclaimer

This book is provided with the understanding that I am not engaging in giving you legal advice, investment or accounting services; just ideas. Specific investment questions should be addressed to a stockbroker, legal questions to a lawyer, and accounting questions to a qualified accountant.

I specifically disclaim any liability, loss, or risk, personal or otherwise, which is incurred as a consequence of any of the contents of this book.

Likewise, you get to keep all profits you make from the use of this book; I don't get any of them.

Contact me via my website or email:

Webpage: www.jjjinvesting.com

E-mail: jeff@jjjinvesting.biz

DEDICATION

To my wonderful honey – bunny (alias lovely wife Judy) who has always been there for me and always will be there for me.

Of course I can't ignore my wonderful wife Judy; again she rates more than just being listed in the dedication. My wonderful wife Judy has been there every step of the way for me and helped me through many dark and difficult times. I truly appreciate all the fine things she's done for me, the love she has for me, the love she has for our daughter and grandchildren, and the hard work she does. I want to give her the best possible life.

TABLE OF CONTENTS

ACKNOWLEDGEMENT

& ADDITIONAL OFFER

For Purchasers of This Book

I would like to thank and compliment Mr. Robert Lichello, author of *How to Make $1,000,000 in the Stock Market Automatically,* who devised the investment system used in my book. I'm sure any good bookstore will have a copy or you could order a copy by looking on Amazon or one of the other websites. Mr. L's book planted a seed of inspiration to me like no other investment book I had ever read. I knew it was the right way to invest. It so inspired me that I started this book and started investing under the system. He has helped lots of people and I hope I am worthy to carry on in his footsteps.

At the time I read the book, the stock market was going great guns in the middle of a big bull market. I started charting stocks I liked under the system to see how well the system worked on real stocks. From those humble beginnings, this book began. It was written under strange conditions about as far away as you can get from the major stock markets – in Seoul, Korea; Maffle, Belgium; and Weilerbach, Germany. The beauty of the system is that it doesn't even require you to be near the market to play. It's so simple and yet so profitable. My hats off to Mr. Lichello. I hope this book helps spread his fine system to an even wider audience.

I wish to make clear that while the system is Mr. Lichello's, the ideas about using it in this book are my own. If you can think of some way to improve on my ideas, I'd be glad to give you credit in a future edition. And now I've come full circle: I've gone from having a printed book for the last 20 years that I've been revising constantly to an e-book version [available for this book]. I've added information on how to adapt Automated Investment Management (AIM) for bear markets, how to invest in the Dogs of the Dow with LEAPS, the safest and best AIM investments for beginning investors, and many other subtle changes. But the heart of the book remains the same because it is a strong heart -- capable of handling the job AIM provides in bull markets and now in bear times.

Anybody who buys this book can e-mail me and will receive for free the full length and full size 8.5 x 11 350-page PDF version of my book. It has all of the spreadsheets so you can go to the particular Chapter and see the spreadsheets that I'm talking about in an easier-to-read version. Once you buy this book, just e-mail me at jeff@jjjinvesting.biz and tell me you have bought my book. I will be very happy to send the full-version book to you at no charge.

As an additional thanks, you will receive a FREE trial subscription to my monthly investing newsletter (a $150 annual value). Contact me to request this free trial to my popular newsletter where I provide several AIM portfolios I track every month, an AIM investing tip of the month, and many other features.

THE INSIGHTFUL STORY
FROM THE 1940 BOOK

"Where Are the Customers' Yachts?"

A banker and a stockbroker take a guest to their yacht club. The guest is very impressed by the beautiful limousine. As they arrive at the yacht club the banker points out the beautiful and expensive building.

The guest says, "Your yacht club is really beautiful!"

The banker says, "That's nothing. Just wait until you see the inside."

The banker, stockbroker, and guest walk inside the yacht club. It is furnished in gorgeous exotic woods, granite, antique stone, and beautiful chandeliers.

The guest is wowed and says, "This is the most beautiful building I've ever seen!"

The stockbroker goes, "Just wait till you see our yachts!"

They walk out the back of the yacht club and start walking down the dock. The guest sees many absolutely spectacular yachts. They walk a little farther and the banker goes: "Look, there is my yacht!"

The guest was very impressed and said, "You have a magnificent boat!"

They walk a little farther and the stockbroker goes, "Look, there is *my* yacht!"

The guest is again awed and tells the stockbroker he really loves his boat.

They walk a little farther down the dock and the guest keeps looking around. Finally he turns to the banker and the stockbroker and says:

"Excuse me, but… where are the *customers'* yachts?"

*****

The point of the story is: **There were no customers' yachts!** The customers weren't earning nearly as much money as the banker and stockbroker.

And yet, the banker and stockbroker were supposed to be helping their customers earn a lot of money, right? But that's not how the normal system works.

Well, read this book and you will learn how to do ***better on your own*** rather than with the actively managed funds. Better than almost any stock trader. Better than any banker who is trying to sell you investments over the phone.

My clients have seen returns of 134% in the last 35 months on the safest and most "conservative" of investments (January 2014 – November 2016 on Dow Jones Dogs of the Dow long-term options).

I believe every person should strive for the highest returns on the safest investments.

Don't you want and deserve this too?

In other words:

Here Are the Customers' Yachts!!

My Short Autobiography

I was born in the Bronx, New York City. I had my first article published in Railroad Model Craftsman (model trains - published in Ramsey, NJ) in July, 1965 when I was 17. I have published my own newsletter for the last twenty years. (http://www.jjjinvesting.com) For over one year, I published a weekly column for Talking Points newsletter entitled *Contrarian Corner*.

I went to college at the University of Arizona and got a Bachelor's Degree in History & Government. Then law school for a year and a half & then to the University of Nevada, Las Vegas for a Bachelor's in Accounting.

I worked for the US Army as an auditor and lived 17 years in Germany, Korea, Japan & Belgium. The ideas for this book came to me in a Godforsaken little town in South Korea 10 miles from the border of North Korea, the DMZ.

My first investing experience:

I was 8 years old living in Ramsey, NJ. I loved railroads and the Erie-Lackawanna Railroad ran right through the middle of town. It was the classic 4-track railroad with the outer tracks for commuter trains to and from New York City and the inner tracks for freight trains.

One day I'm reading my dad's New York Journal-American newspaper. I look at the New York Stock Market stock listings and see that Erie-Lackawanna is a stock. And it's selling for $2.62. I think to myself that I have $300 in a savings account paying about 1% interest (just like today).

In those days you usually had to buy stocks in 100 share lots. I go to my dad and tell him I want to take the money out of the savings account and buy 100 shares of Erie-Lackawanna. Unfortunately my dad grew up during the Great Depression and could only see the negatives in the stock market. I argued and argued but my dad wouldn't let me buy the stock.

I forgot all about this until Christmas. My dad totally surprised me with a model train set set up on a Ping-Pong table in our basement. I went to check my Christmas stocking and was totally amazed to find out my dad somehow had managed to buy me 5 shares of Erie-Lackawanna. How he did this I'll never know. So now I'm the proud owner of 5 shares of Erie-Lackawanna!

Next summer I find out that the Penn Central Railroad bought out Erie-Lackawanna. Penn Central redeemed every share of Erie-Lackawanna for $16 a share. I get a check in the mail for $80. That was great! I realized if I had bought the 100 shares of Erie-Lackawanna I would have received a check for $1,600 – all the money in the world to an 8 year old!

That taught me a valuable lesson that there is money to be made in the stock market. I am sharing with you an easy way to make high profits for life in the stock market with this book.

Jeffrey Weber in San Antonio, Texas, USA

INTRODUCTION

I wrote my book to help all investors – big and small – make money. The simple, easy to learn system will show you an investment method you can use for life. It only takes an hour once a month and should average more than 20% – 30% a year over the long haul.

In addition to showing you the investing system, I will show you how to choose a stockbroker for buying and selling under the AIM system (in the full-length book version). To help you pick the best stocks, I offer a monthly HTML newsletter. Email me at jeff@jjjinvesting.biz for further details. Anybody who buys a copy of my e-book will receive a free trial subscription to my monthly investing newsletter. It shows the best long-term options (LEAPS), ETF's, and closed-end funds for the AIM system. Email me to ask for your free trial subscription to my newsletter now that you have purchased this book.

Please read the entire book and I think you'll agree that I offer a simple, easy to learn, quick method to make the most profits from your hard-earned investment dollars. A note on the examples – some of them use data from a few years ago. These come from my full-length book and are still valid today. AIM worked then and the same process works today because this is a system to make profits over a lifetime.

It also doesn't take very much money to get started as you'll see. If you have any questions, I'll be glad to try and answer them. Please e-mail me. Good luck with your investing.

How the Stock Market Works

(Condensed Version)

Businesses issue shares of stock to raise capital for their businesses. Investors buy the shares of stock. Then investors trade the stocks on Stock Exchanges. This trading causes the stock prices to go up and down.

Many stocks also have options. Options give the buyer the right but not the obligation to buy shares of the stock at a set Strike Price. Options are more volatile than stocks and thus their prices will go up and down faster than the corresponding stock price. But when used systematically and safely – as this book will explain for you – they can be just as safe as the stock they represent. Plus they are much cheaper than the stock price so you can control many more shares. The volatility and increased number of shares make them perfect for our AIM investing system.

Options can expire in one month or over two years depending on their expiration date. We will only use long-term options (LEAPS) which expire two years in the future. For instance, the 2019 LEAPS roll out in December 2016. During 2017 you would purchase or roll over to 2019 LEAPS for our Dogs of the Dow portfolio.

CHAPTER 1

Need for LEAPS & AIM & Dogs of the Dow

I am going to show you an investing method that is very safe and makes high profits (up 143% last 34 months as I write this in November 2016). In order to make the high profits and keep the investing method we need to use two things: LEAPS & AIM. But the first thing you need to do is open a stock broker account. And when you open it you need to tell your broker you want to be able to buy and sell (trade) options. You only need low level option approval which is routinely granted after you read the booklet warning you of the dangers of trading options. Email me with any questions after you read this book – jeff@jjjinvesting.biz

LEAPS

LEAPS are long-term options that expire the 3rd Friday in any given January and have more than one year before they expire. LEAPS are issued every September, October & November for the next year. By the end of November all the new LEAPS that will expire on the third Friday of January 2019 will be issued. Every January I sell the old LEAPS and buy the new LEAPS for the Dogs of the Dow LEAPS portfolio.

So in January I will look at the Dogs of the Dow web page listed in my newsletter and see what the current 10 Dogs of the Dow are for 2017. Some of the previous years' Dogs may change.

Then I will look up long-term options (LEAPS) prices for the January 2019 LEAPS. To find these prices on Yahoo.com go to Yahoo Finance and type the stocks symbol – for example Caterpillar has the symbol CAT. When the summary page comes up, click on the hot link for options. The options with the shortest expiration date will appear. We don't want these options – click on the date button and you will see a drop-down menu of different dates – the options (LEAPS) we want are near or at the bottom. Now click on Jan 2019 and the LEAPS that expire in January 2019 will appear. Now we only want to look at the Call prices (Calls mean you are bullish on the stock and think it will go higher)

Now we have to choose a Strike Price. The Strike Price is the amount you could buy 100 shares at any time up till the LEAPS expire in January 2019. We are only trading the LEAPS contracts – we will never take delivery of the stock – that is for a different type of investor. I recommend picking a Strike Price at or near what the stock is selling at. For example, if Caterpillar is selling at 80, then pick a Strike Price of 80 or 85. You want to be able to buy around 10 contracts so you will be able to trade contracts and make money. The amount of money you will be starting with will determine what LEAP price you should buy.

For example – if you have $10,000 then you will buy $5,000 worth of LEAPS so you can buy 10 contracts at $500 each (Yahoo Finance shows price of one option is $5, so it costs $500 to buy one contract – all contracts have 100 options.

In another example if you have $3,000 then you will buy $1,500 worth of LEAPS so you can buy 10 contracts at $300 each. Option prices get lower the more Out of the Money the option is. So if the stock price is $50, the Strike 50 option might be $5, the Strike 60 option might be $3, the Strike 70 option might be $1.

2

This gets a little complicated for beginners so I invite you to hire me for 6 months of educational services to help you manage your portfolio after you get started and show you how to trade using my AIM system for 6 months. Then you will thoroughly understand this investing method and easily be able to do it yourself. Of course I am happy to continue helping you with your portfolio. Again I am trying to give you enough information so you know when you need to ask me a question. Everybody has a different level of investing knowledge. I don't want investing novices to be scared – this is easy to learn with my help and will make you very high profits on very safe investments.

I ask new investors to focus more on the rest of my book and see just how high the profits are. Once you are convinced this is a good, safe way to invest, then I want you to come to me for help, have me help you get started and manage your account. You will see in Chapter 4 how to buy and sell using my investing system.

AIM

AIM stands for Automatic Investment Management. This is an investing method invented by Robert Lichello over 30 years ago. It's a very simple investing method that tells exactly when to buy, when to sell, and when to do nothing. This is an investing method that guarantees you **Buy Low and Sell High**. I won't go into more detail here because AIM is fully explained in Chapter 4 – The Mechanics of Buying and Selling.

Dogs of the Dow

The Dogs of the Dow are the 10 of the 30 Dow Jones Industrial Average Stocks that pay the highest dividends. I have the links to the Dogs of the Dow web site in my monthly newsletter – the main page is www.dogsofthedow.com. We want to buy LEAPS on these stocks because they are very safe AND will make up very high profits over the long haul – as of October 2016 the Dogs of the Dow LEAPS portfolio is up 143% in 34 months. See Chapter 7 for more information on Dogs of the Dow stocks.

CHAPTER 2

Why the AIM System Works

A check of the share price of Campbell Resources (spreadsheet found in full-version book) shows it has declined from the original price of $6.00 a share to $2.37 a share or a 61% drop. Thus a lump sum investor (all money is in the stock), if he or she had invested the same total amount of money you had (in total $35,000), would've lost 61% and the $35,000 investment would have lost $21,350 and be worth $13,650 in November 1987. Compare that to what your investment is now worth. **Your total portfolio is worth $48,610 up from the total of $35,000 you invested; quite good for stock that may be a total disaster. You're ahead $13,610 or 38.8%.** How do we do it? What's the trick? Why does the system work?

THREE REASONS FOR AIM PROFITS

Reason 1: I was curious myself and so I started investigating. A review of the buy/sell chart at the end of the chapter shows that your average buy price (excluding initial buy) was $1.35. Your average sale price was $1.95. Thus you made $.60 per share profit on every share you sold.

You sold 13,000 X $.60 = $7,856

Reason 2: Some profit comes from interest earned on the cash balance (add column 10) = $1,120.

Reason 3: The rest of the profit comes from the increase in value of your remaining shares of stock. I won't give all the details but will show you a couple of examples: you buy 5,771 shares at $.94 each and 5,291 shares at $.87 each. As of September 1987, the share price for Campbell Resources is $2.37. Each of the 5,771 shares is worth $1.43 more than what you paid for it or 5,771 X $1.43 = $8,252 more. Each of the 5,291 shares is worth $1.50 more than you paid for it or 5,291 X $1.50 = $7,937 more. If you check the buy sheet, you'll see other months where you bought stock for less than the current $2.37 share price.

When you see that you can make money on a stock that drops 61% below your original purchase price, you know you have a really amazing system. Of course you had to have a fairly tough attitude to hang in there and put that extra $25,000 into the stock. Think of the profits if Campbell Resources merely goes back to its original selling price. Or if you decide to get out, sellout; you can sell all your shares, take your profit, and get into another stock. The choice is yours.

See the Campbell Resources full-size spreadsheets below and in your free full-length PDF book available for free by emailing me at jeff@jjjinvesting.biz. Also, see my chapter on using Bear Strategy with LEAPS in my full-size book version (350 pages long!) and in Chapter 5 of this book. To see the Campbell spreadsheet with AIM, send for my free full-version book at jeff@jjjinvesting.biz. And don't forget to ask for your free trial of my newsletter.

PROOF YOU BUY LOW, SELL HIGH, AND MAKE PROFITS WITH AIM							
CAMPBELL RESOURCES							
	BUYS			SELLS			PORT-FOLIO VALUE
DATE	SHARE PRICE	# OF SHARES	TOTAL SPENT	SHARE PRICE	# OF SHARES	TOTAL REC'D	
Jan-85	$4.12	394	$1,625				$7,968
2–5/85	similar	none	none		none	none	$8,936
Jun-85	$3.12	738	$2,306				$8,796
Jul-85	$3.25	189	$613				$8,796
Aug-85	$3.37	none	none		none	none	$9,105
Sep-85	$2.87	434	$1,238				$9,893
Oct-85	$2.12	1348	$2,864				$9,751
Nov-85	$2.25	251	$565				$10,283
12/85-1/86	similar	none	none		none	none	$10,842
Feb-86	$2.12	619	$1,316				$11,727
Mar-86	$1.87	1026	$1,924				$12,461
Apr-86	$1.25	3977	$4,971				$13,647
May-86	$0.94	5774	$5,428				$15,520
Jun-86	$0.87	3779	$3,307				$18,491
Jul-86	$0.87	1512	$1,323				$19,498
Aug-86	$1.25			$1.25	2,326	$2,908	$27,435
Sep-86	$1.50			$1.50	3,019	$4,528	$32,167
10/11/86	similar	none	none		none	none	$30,270
Dec-86	$1.12	1180	$1,327				$26,361

Continued…

| | BUYS | | | SELLS | | | PORT-FOLIO VALUE |
DATE	SHARE PRICE	# OF SHARES	TOTAL SPENT	SHARE PRICE	# OF SHARES	TOTAL REC'D	
Jan-87	$1.12	472	531				$26,397
Feb-87	$1.37	none	none		none	none	$30,796
Mar-87	$1.62			$1.62	2,287	$3,716	$35,205
Apr-87	$2.62			$2.62	5,344	$14,027	$50,430
May-87	$2.25	none	none		none	none	$46,866
Jun-87	$2.25	none	none		none	none	$46,990
Jul-87	$2.25	none	none		none	none	$47,115
Aug-87	$2.50			$2.50	118	$295	$49,697
Sep-87	$2.37	none	none		none	none	$48,610
TOTAL		21,693	$29,338		13,094	$25,474	$48,610

AVG. BUY PRICE = $1.35   AVG. SELL PRICE = $1.95

Notice the average difference of $0.60 a share on 13,094 shares sold => Buying low and selling high created $7,856.40 profit!

CHAPTER 3

The Safest Way to Invest with AIM

I updated this chapter in October 2016. When you read my newsletter you will see seven model portfolios. The best one for novice investors, who like safety, spending only 2 hours once a month, and having profits of 143% in 34 months as of October 2016, is the Dogs of the Dow long-term options (LEAPS) portfolio.

LEAPS are totally explained in chapters near the end of the book. Sixty thousand dollars starting in January 2014 has grown to $143,611 as of October 2016. See two examples of the two Dogs stocks on the following pages (I don't show all 10 because my book would just be too long.) The first is CAT (Caterpillar) and the second is XOM (Exxon Mobile). Each stock started with $6,000: $3,000 worth of LEAPS & $3,000 worth of CASH in Jan 2014 – I am only showing the latest results starting in January 2016. Remember, each of these examples started with $3,000 of LEAPS & $3,000 of cash in January 2014.

Just in the first 9 months of 2016, using the AIM system with both of these stocks, their portfolios values have almost doubled. Look at the last column in the tables below which shows the total portfolio value (PORT VALUE). You'll learn what the other columns mean and how to use them in the next Chapter.

DATE	REMARK CAT Jan 18 S 65	SHARE PRICE	SHARE VALUE	SAFE	CASH	Contracts BOUGHT (SOLD)	SHARES OWNED	PORT CONTROL	BUY (SELL) ADVICE	MKT ORD (SELL) BUY	6 % INT	# of Conts	PORT VALUE
1/8/16		7.25	5075	507	4774	-	700	5075	-	-	24	7	9,873
2/9/16		8.70	6090	609	4798	-	700	5075	(1015)	Ign (406)	24	7	10,888
3/9/16		12.50	8790	875	4822	(2)	700	5075	(3675)	(2500)	24	5	13,572
4/11/16		13.05	6525	652	7359	-	500	5075	(1450)	Ign (798)	37	5	13,884
5/9/16		11.20	5600	560	7396	-	500	5075	(525)	-	37	5	12,996
6/9/16		14.50	7250	725	7434	(1)	500	5075	(2175)	(1450)	38	4	14,684
7/18/16		14.75	5900	590	8928	-	400	5075	(825)	Ign (235)	44	4	14,828
8/9/16		20.01	8004	800	8973	(1)	400	5075	(2929)	(2001)	45	3	16,977

DATE	REMARK Exxon Mobile XOM Jan 18 75	SHARE PRICE	SHARE VALUE	SAFE	CASH	CONTRT BOUGHT (SOLD)	SHARES OWNED	PORT CONTROL	BUY (SELL) ADVICE	MKT ORD (SELL) BUY	6 % INT	# of Contracts	PORT VALUE
1/8/16		9.05	6335	633	5804	-	700	6335	-	-	-	7	12,168
2/9/16		4.70	3290	329	5833	6	700	6335	3045	2820	29	13	9,123
3/9/16		13.35	17355	1735	3028	(6)	1300	7745	(9610)	(8010)	15	7	20,383
4/11/16		12.00	8400	840	11093	-	700	7745	(655)	-	55	7	19,493
5/9/16		15.45	10815	1081	11149	(1)	700	7745	(3070)	(1545)	56	6	21,964
6/9/16		17.40	10440	1044	12757	(1)	600	7745	(2695)	(1740)	63	5	23,197
7/8/16		20.15	10075	1007	14569	-	500	7745	(2330)	Ign (1323)	72	5	24,644
8/9/16		15.50	7750	775	14642	-	500	7745	(5)	-	73	5	22,392

10

CHAPTER 4

The Mechanics of Buying and Selling

Now for how to buy, sell, or do nothing under the (Automatic Investment Management) AIM system. This is an important -- probably the most important -- chapter of the book. You must thoroughly understand and follow this to get the benefits from the AIM system. I'm going to go through it slowly and I want you not only to read and understand it, but also practice it with some stocks of your own until it becomes second nature. And it will! At first it might seem complicated, but it's really incredibly simple. And once you learn it you will be doing exactly the same process every month but the results will be different. Some months the AIM system will tell you to buy and it will tell you how much to buy or how many dollars' worth of the investment to buy or how many dollars' worth of the investment to sell or AIM may want you to do nothing because the price of the investment hasn't gone down or up enough for AIM to decide to make a buy or sell. Here's how to do it.

You will see that this example comes from a while ago. Don't worry about the particular year – the way AIM works is timeless so this is still a good example. As long as prices are moving up or down or holding steady the AIM system tells you to buy or sell and how much to buy and sell or do nothing. This stays the same year after year. When you subscribe to my monthly newsletter you will get the very latest numbers in several portfolios and you will see that the AIM system is still earning great profits after all these years. Imagine if you had started using this system back when this example came from. Don't have the same regret 20 years from now.

There still may be some old-fashioned investors who don't like computers so this will appeal to them. I have created a paper version of the spreadsheet. If you use a computer spreadsheet you can make it easier by putting in a few very simple formulas in some of the columns.

Email me at jeff@jjjinvesting.biz. I will send you a blank sheet for stocks and a separate blank spreadsheet with headings for long-term options (LEAPS). I recommend you print out the blank spreadsheet, copy the first row from the finished spreadsheet, and then copy the date and share price columns. Then do the Claire's Stores spreadsheet yourself. When you get the same numbers as the printed spreadsheet you understand how to do AIM.

Now a quick explanation of what every column means before we look at two years of one stock and you see the system in action.

Column 1 DATE - The date becomes the month and year (for example 6/16.) You check your stock or LEAP at least once a month or more often if you wish. It might be daily for some of the more volatile investments like LEAPs or leveraged ETF's. In this example I am just going to be checking the stock monthly. And you will see just checking it monthly can still make you quite a nice profit. So 6/16 would be followed by 7/16, followed by 8/16 - I think you get the picture.

Column 2 REMARKS - Here you will list things such as readjust stock/cash ratio, stock splits using different SAFE percent's (10% is the normal SAFE amount as you'll see later on) but we will use different SAFE percentages in bear markets.

Column 3 – SHARE PRICE - This is the closing price of one long-term option (LEAPS) as reported in the newspaper or the website for the day you're checking. You can easily find daily prices at

12

http://yahoo.com in the financial section or if you have an iPhone you can find websites that will list option prices.

Column 4 – SHARE VALUE - This is the SHARE PRICE from column 3 multiplied by the number of SHARES OWNED which is found in column 8.

Column 5 SAFE – SAFE is an arbitrary 10% of the share value found in column 2. Thus, if your SHARE VALUE is $5,000, your SAFE amount would be $500. You'll see how SAFE keeps you from buying and selling too soon when we go through the actual example stock.

Column 6 – CASH - Originally Robert Lichello said to use a ratio of 50% CASH and 50% shares when you start an AIM investment. So for example, if you started with $10,000, you would have $5,000 in options, and $5,000 in CASH. I have found that we can vary the amount of cash in an AIM investment depending on the volatility of the investment. A quick example is on a LEAP which is a very volatile investment; you would always want to use a ratio of 50% CASH and 50% LEAPs. And on a closed-end fund that you buy for income, you can safely use a ratio of one third CASH and two thirds closed-end fund shares that would mean on a $10,000 investment, you could own $6,677 worth of closed-end fund shares and $3,333 for CASH.

One disadvantage nowadays of keeping a great amount of cash in your broker's money market account, is that money market accounts pay a very low interest rate, usually less than 1%. This means you're not earning very much on the money but having cash to buy shares at cheaper prices is an essential that will pay off for you later on when your stock or other investment goes down and you need to buy more shares. I have found a way you can make high interest on your

CASH balance – put your CASH money into High-Yielding Closed-End Funds like AGNC which pays a monthly dividend and pays more than 6% dividend per year. There are other good high yielding closed-end funds also.

Your CASH total will go up or down every month depending on whether you're buying and selling and earning interest on your cash. Also I view it as optional if you want to deduct the cost of the commissions as you make buys and sells. Personally I wouldn't bother worrying about the commissions; you make enough profits without really worrying about it.

You'll see that the AIM system is very conservative as half of your investment will go to CASH. If you have a buy, then Column 6 (CASH) – Column 11 (MARKET ORDER BUY) X 1.005 (interest) equals next month's cash total. If you have a sell, then, Column 6 + Column 11 (MARKER ORDER (SELL) x 1.005 equals next month's cash total.

Column 7 – SHARES BOUGHT (SOLD) - After you make your monthly check of the option price investment price, you might be buying some options, selling some options or doing nothing. In this column you will record the number of long-term option (LEAPS) contracts you bought or sold for that particular day in time. If you did nothing, put a – (dash) in the column. To arrive at the number of option contracts you bought or sold, you divide the dollar amount in column 11 (MARKET ORDER BOUGHT (SOLD)) by the option SHARE PRICE in column 3. For example, if the system tells you to sell 3 contracts (300 options) and the LEAPS contracts are selling for $350, then you sell 3 contracts for $1,050. Remember to put the "( )" around the sold contracts to keep separate the buy and sell transactions which are sharing the same column.

Column 8 – SHARES OWNED - This is the number of option shares you currently own. This figure will constantly go up and down. Column 8 equals last month's column 8 plus any option contracts you bought in the previous month minus any option contracts sold in the previous month or day that you did AIM. If the previous month or day that you did AIM and AIM told you don't need to make any buys or sells; then column 8 would be the same number of option shares in the row just above the current row you're using.

Column 9 PORTFOLIO CONTROL – This is another important column. When you start, put a dollar amount equal to the dollar amount of option contracts you bought to start (this is only a control number, no money involved with this column). If you start with $1,000 worth of options, your PORTFOLIO CONTROL amount/number is also 1,000. After your initial injection of money, PORTFOLIO CONTROL will only change if you buy more options. Every time you buy more, you add half the amount you bought to your PORTFOLIO CONTROL total. For example, the system tells you to buy $800 worth of option contracts; you add $400 to your prior PORTFOLIO CONTROL total. If no buy, then column 9 is the same as the prior month.

Column 10 – BUY (SELL) ADVICE - Every month you look at your option SHARE VALUE (column 4) and PORTFOLIO CONTROL. If your option SHARE VALUE is higher, you put that figure on top; if your PORTFOLIO CONTROL amount is higher, you put that on top. For example: if your option SHARE VALUE is $5,000 and your PORTFOLIO CONTROL amount is higher, you put PORTFOLIO CONTROL on top. For example: if you're option SHARE VALUE IS $5,000 and your PORTFOLIO CONTROL is $3,000 then you would put the higher value on top like this:

SHARE VALUE	$5,000
- PORTFOLIO CONTROL	3,000
= (SELL) ADVICE	$2,000

Or if PORTFOLIO CONTROL is higher:

PORTFOLIO CONTROL	$5,000
- SHARE VALUE	$3,000
= BUY ADVICE	$2,000

Column 11 – MARKET ORDER BUY (SELL) - This is the column that tells you whether you execute an order with your stock broker or not. You take the amount from column 10, BUY (SELL) ADVICE, and subtract out the SAFE (column 5) amount. If the amount is over $300 (this is my new rule of thumb for determining when you make actual buys or sells for options.) This means you go online and tell your broker that you want to buy or sell the dollar amount of your MARKET ORDER by telling the broker the number of long-term option (LEAPS) contracts you want to buy or sell. If you have a sell order, you have to figure out how many option contracts you must sell (column 11 divided by column 3, SHARE PRICE X 100) and tell your broker to sell that many contracts. For example, if your market order was to sell $300 worth of $100 option contract, then you would tell your broker to sell 3 contracts. You would do the same exact thing if it's a buy order, you divide the dollar amount of the buy order by the current price of the option and that determines how many contracts you buy. Always remember investing is an art and not a science, so if the AIM system tells you to buy 2.7 contracts, then you can easily round that off to buy 3 contracts and everything will work fine.

COLUMN 12 – 6% INTEREST - This is the amount of interest earned by your cash total from column 6. The .005 is 1/12 of 6% or the amount of interest you earn in one month. I picked 6% because it's easy to work with over a long period of time. It is a fair average of the interest rate you can earn on high-yield closed-end funds over the long-term and it keeps things simple; monthly interest is always one half of 1%. Remember we are in this for the long haul and if you play AIM over the next 20-30 years, your high-yield closed-end funds will average out to 6% interest. I can help you to earn the 6% by buying High Yield Closed-End funds that pay 6% or higher with your Cash.

Column 13 – PORTFOLIO VALUE/TOTAL - Add the value of your CASH, column 6 + SHARE VALUE column 4, the value of your options or other investment and you have the total current value of your investment. You will notice one nice thing about the AIM spreadsheet. Once you start with the stock you see exactly what you're starting amount is in the very first row when you look at PORTFOLIO TOTAL. In this example we are starting with a PORTFOLIO TOTAL of $10,000. And then in future months you can see how much you are ahead in profits!

So when you compare PORTFOLIO TOTALs in the future rows, you can easily see exactly what your status is, if the PORTFOLIO TOTAL is higher than $10,000 then you are ahead or profitable. If the PORTFOLIO TOTAL is less than $10,000, you currently have a "paper loss". All that means is that the option or other investment is cheaper than when you originally bought it, and possibly AIM is telling you to buy more option shares of this cheap option so when it turns around and goes higher later on you will own more option shares that will go up in value and that will increase your profits.

Now I will go through an actual stock (long-term options hadn't been invented yet) and show you just how easy it is. Get your pencil, calculator, and 13 – column paper or spreadsheet. Write all the headings in the proper columns. Now write the name of the stock, for this example I picked Claire's Stores (CLE), see the completed spreadsheet at the end of this Chapter. Then below the name list the stock exchange. NYSE equals the New York Stock Exchange. The first month in our example is June 1994 (6/94), write that in your date column. Then we are going to imagine that we have $10,000 to invest. Having a calculator will make your figuring easier. We are going to start with June 1994 because that is when I made this example. The numbers would be different today of course but the process is the same.

The first month is June 94 (6/94), write that in your date column. Then we are going to imagine that we have $10,000 to invest. Having a calculator or using formulas in the spreadsheet will make your figuring easier.

JUNE 1994

Date Col. 1	Remarks Col. 2	Share Price Col. 3	Share Value Col. 4	SAFE Col. 5	Cash Col. 6	Shares Bought (Sold) Col. 7	Shares Owned Col. 8	Port Control Col. 9	Buy (Sell) Advice Col. 10	Mrk Order (Sell) Buy Col. 11	6% Int Col 12	Port Value Col 13
6/94		10.25	6700	670	3300	-	654	6700	-	-	-	-	10,000

18

We start with $10,000 to invest. First we look at the price of the stock or option in the newspaper or on the website. A great website to look up stock prices is Yahoo Finance - all you have to do is type in the symbol and you'll see exactly what the current price of any stock or options is. When you actually buy your stock or option, you'll be able to go your account online and see what price you paid. For the original buy price we will use a limit price so we know what price we paid.

LEAPS prices and stock prices can move quickly so you may have put in an online order to say buy Claire's Stores and Yahoo told you the price was $10.25. You might find when you actually buy it maybe you bought the stock at $10.20 or $10.30 so that is the price you would want to put down when you find your actual buy price. Our stock was selling for $10.25. Write that in column 3. Our first share value will be 2/3 of our $10,000 or $6,700 rounded off. **For very conservative stocks we can go 2/3 stock & 1/3 cash but for long-term options (LEAPS) like we use with the Dogs of the Dow stocks we always go 50% LEAPS, 50% Cash.** Write $6,700 in column 4. In this example you see I used the liberal idea of two thirds stock and one third cash. Based on the investment you are going to be in (Dogs of the Dow LEAPS) I will recommend that you go 50% cash and 50% long-term options (LEAPS.)

Then in column 5, write $670 because SAFE is always 10% of the SHARE VALUE, in column 4. Then write $3,300 in column 6 because you always start with two thirds of your money in stock and one third in cash on a conservative investment. In column 8 you write the number of shares you own. This is figured by dividing SHARE VALUE in column 4 by the SHARE PRICE – in column 3 - $10.25 equals 654 shares. Always round off, if you get 653.9, then 654 shares, if 653.3, then 653 shares. Then in column 9 PORTFOLIO CONTROL, put in the same number as you had in column 4, SHARE VALUE, 6,700.

Column 10 doesn't come into play yet, and column 11 doesn't either. You haven't earned any interest yet, so column 12 is blank also. Now add up the value of the stock you bought in column 4 and the amount of cash in column 6 and you have your total for PORTFOLIO VALUE. Put $6,700 + $3,300 equals $10,000.

Now let me show you how simple and profitable the system will be for you. Remember to reinvest all dividends into your money market account or closed-end high yield funds. Just tell your broker when you open your account that you always want any dividends placed into your money market account and you do not want to buy additional shares or fractions of shares with any dividends you receive. **You will not have this problem with long-term options (LEAPS) because they do not pay dividends on options – only shares of stock or closed-end funds pay dividends.**

JULY 1994

Date Col. 1	Remarks Col. 2	Share Price Col. 3	Share Value Col. 4	SAFE Col. 5	Cash Col. 6	Shares Bought (Sold) Col. 7	Shares Owned Col. 8	Port Control Col. 9	Buy (Sell) Advice Col. 10	Mrk Order (Sell) Buy Col. 11	6% Int Col 12	Comm	Port Value Col 13
6/94		10.25	6700	670	3300	-	654	6700	-	-	-	-	10,000
7/94		10.00	6540	654	3317	-	654	6700	160	-	17	-	9,857

Now how to use the system in the real world. On July 1 or thereabouts, you pick up your newspaper or look on your computer. You type in the symbol and find Claire's Stores. From now on I'm just going to say you look on your computer because when I wrote this, newspapers were a lot greater source of stock market information than they are today.

20

Today everything you want is either on a website or your iPhone on your iPad etc. so now on we would just say we look it up on the web. My new iPhone has this great little feature; all I have to do is press the stock market app on the very opening screen and I can find out all the information on stock prices you ever dreamed of. You can always find any symbol by going to Yahoo Finance. Barrons has information on stocks at http://www.barrons.com. Go down to the bottom and open up either the New York or NASDAQ stock exchange. Go to the first letter of the stock's name and you will see the symbol right next to the name of the stock.

We find Claire's Stores and see that the price on July 1 is $10, which we write in column 3. Did you remember to put July, 94, - 7/94, in the date column? Now go to column 8 for July 94. Look above in column 8 and you will see you owned 654 shares in June and you didn't buy or sell any in column 7. This is why you leave column 7 blank in the first month. You still own 654 shares. Write 654 in column 8 for July 94.

Also your PORTFOLIO CONTROL amount is still the same (you didn't buy anything in addition to the opening buy in the first month, when you opened your account), so write 6,700 in column 9. Now multiply the number of shares owned (654) by the share price ($10) and you have your SHARE VALUE for column 4. Now CASH, you'll notice, has grown from $3,300 to $3,317. This is because you earned $17 interest (1/2 of 1% for a month) which you write in column 12. If you had bought or sold stocks the preceding month, that would have also affected cash this month.

Now you take your two key amounts – SHARE VALUE and PORTFOLIO CONTROL and look at them. Which is higher? PORTFOLIO CONTROL is higher (6,700) than SHARE VALUE (6,540). Since PORTFOLIO CONTROL is higher, put PORTFOLIO CONTROL on top. You'll be seeing this chart every month. Once you start doing this, you won't need the chart, but it's a good way to learn.

PORTFOLIO CONTROL	6,700
- SHARE VALUE	$6,540
= BUY ADVICE	$160

You now have a potential buy for $160 but it's only potential. Now look at the SAFE amount in column 5 and you find that it is 654 which is higher than your buyer advice in column 10. So you put zero in column 11, MARKET ORDER BUY because your signal isn't strong enough to give you a market order yet. Put a "–" (dash) in column 7 since you won't be buying or selling any stock this month. Be patient, the system doesn't want you to sell or buy too soon. You'll get plenty of chances. Now all you have to do is figure column 13, PORTFOLIO VALUE. You remember, add column 4, SHARE VALUE and column 6, CASH and you have the current value of your investment. This month it's $6,540 + $3,317 = $9,857. If the stock goes up in price, you'll have a potential sell and if it goes down, a potential buy.

Now for August 94. I'll be shorter in my explanations and you'll see you will still understand because you did the same thing every month. While every month is done the same, the outcome can be quite different.

AUGUST 1994

Date Col. 1	Remarks Col. 2	Share Price Col. 3	Share Value Col. 4	SAFE Col. 5	Cash Col. 6	Shares Bought (Sold) Col. 7	Shares Owned Col. 8	Port Control Col. 9	Buy (Sell) Advice Col. 10	Mrk Order (Sell) Buy Col. 11	6% Int Col 12	Comm	Port Value Col 13
7/94		10.00	6540	654	3317	-	654	6700	160	-	17	-	9,857
8/94		12.37	8093	809	3334	(47)	654	6700	(1393)	(584)	17	-	11,427

First look up the price of Claire's stock. Claire's price is $12.37. Write in column 3. Then multiply the number of shares owned (still 654 shares since you didn't buy or sell any last month) by the price of one share and that gives you a SHARE VALUE of $8,093. SAFE is always 10% so write 809 in column 5. Again the only thing that affected CASH is INTEREST; you earned another $17. So write $17 in column 12 and add $17 to your CASH. You now have $3,334 in CASH. Since you didn't buy any stock last month, PORTFOLIO CONTROL stays the same at 6,700. The magic two numbers are SHARE VALUE and PORTFOLIO CONTROL. Again, since SHARE VALUE is higher, put that on top. Since SHARE VALUE is higher, you have a potential (sell) signal; now write the higher amount SHARE VALUE on top:

SHARE VALUE	$8,093 (COL. 4)
- PORTFOLIO CONTROL	6,700 (COL. 9)
= (SELL) ADVICE	$1,393 (COL. 10)
Now subtract SAFE from (SELL) ADVICE	- 809 (COL.5)
= MARKET ORDER (SELL)	$ 584 (COL.11)

You should be writing all these figures on your sample spreadsheet the same as the illustration at the end of the Chapter shows.

As you can see, you're getting your first sell order. Now divide $584 by the SHARE PRICE ($12.37) and you have 47 shares to sell. Write (47) in SHARES BOUGHT (SOLD) column. Now finish your months' work by figuring out your PORTFOLIO VALUE. It's ($8,093) + column 6 ($3,334) = $11,427. Now you call your stockbroker or go to your online trading account and execute a sell for 47 shares.

You're ahead $1,427 but better things are still ahead.

Now let's go even quicker because I'm sure you understand how simple and repetitive the system is and soon you'll see its power. Try doing September '94 on your own. Remember to start by looking up the price of Claire's Stores. Since this is an example, of course you can't but soon you'll be doing your own stocks and this will be the first step.

SEPTEMBER 1994

Date Col. 1	Remarks Col. 2	Share Price Col. 3	Share Value Col. 4	SAFE Col. 5	Cash Col. 6	Shares Bought (Sold) Col. 7	Shares Owned Col. 8	Port Control Col. 9	Buy (Sell) Advice Col. 10	Mrk Order (Sell) Buy Col. 11	6% Int Col 12	Comm	Port Value Col 13
8/94		12.37	8093	809	3334	(47)	654	6700	(1393)	(584)	17	·	11,427
9/94		12.50	7588	758	3938	(10)	607	6700	(888)	(130)	20	·	11,526

Okay, the price has risen and is now $12.50. Write down $12.50 and then fill in column 9 that didn't change since no buying last month. But column 8, SHARES OWNED, did change. We sold 47 shares last month. So subtract 47 from the column 8 total from the prior month (654 - 47 = 607). Write 607 in column 8, SHARES OWNED. Now figure column 6 CASH. You started with $3,334 and must add the $584 you got from selling the stock. So $3,334+ $584 = $3,918 + $20 for INTEREST = $3,938, WRITE in column 6, CASH. Write $20 in column 12, INTEREST.

Then compare column 4 with column 9 and see which is higher. SHARE VALUE is still higher $7,588 To PORTFOLIO CONTROL's 6,700. You can figure you have a potential (SELL) of $888 that you write in column 10. You glance at SAFE and see its lower than your potential (SELL) ADVICE (888-758 = 130), so you write (130) in column 11, MARKET ORDER (SELL) BUY. You have a sell. Now divide $130 by $12.50 and you find you sell 10 shares. In this example I am making any sells over $100. Many years later I have decided that is too low because it generates too many commissions and so I've basically raised the amount of any buy or sell to a minimum of $300 so you would pay fewer commissions and sell at higher prices and buy at lower prices. Write

25

(10) in column 7, SHARES BOUGHT (SOLD). Add up the value of your portfolio in column 13 – remember it's CASH + SHARE VALUE. Your PORTFOLIO VALUE is $11,526.

OCTOBER 1994

Date Col. 1	Remark Col. 2	Share Price Col. 3	Share Value Col. 4	SAFE Col. 5	Cash Col. 6	Shares Bought (Sold) Col. 7	Shares Owned Col. 8	Port Control Col. 9	Buy (Sell) Advice Col. 10	Mrk Order (Sell) Buy Col. 11	6% Int Col 12	Comm	Port Value Col 13
9/94		12.50	7588	758	3938	(10)	607	6700	(888)	(130)	20	-	11,526
10/94		11.00	6567	656	4088	-	597	6700	133	-	20	-	10,655

Now October '94. Stock price is $11.00 (stock prices do go down). Again write the SHARES OWNED and PORTFOLIO CONTROL numbers in columns 8 and 9. Column 9, PORTFOLIO CONTROL hasn't changed since no buying but SHARES OWNED did change since we sold 10 shares. So go to last month's column 8 total and subtract 10 (607-10 = 597) and write that number in column 8. Now figure SHARE VALUE and you see it's less than $6,700. It's $6,567 to be exact. SAFE is always 10% of SHARE VALUE so fill that in. CASH again was affected by selling. You started with $3,938 and added $130 + $20 INTEREST = $4,088.

Now look at PORTFOLIO CONTROL and it is higher than SHARE VALUE so put PORTFOLIO CONTROL on top. Think P for purchase. You have BUY ADVICE of $133. Before you do anything, you still must compare BUY ADVICE to SAFE. SAFE is going to cancel this market order because it is greater than the BUY ADVICE.

Did you remember **not** to put ( ) around zero in column 11? I don't bother putting ( ) around 0 in column 11, I just use a –. Again if you

26

haven't given yourself $20 in INTEREST, add $20 to your CASH account and again add SHARE VALUE and CASH to obtain your PORTFOLIO VALUE. Your PORTFOLIO VALUE is $10,655.

NOVEMBER 1994

Date Col. 1	Remark Col. 2	Share Price Col. 3	Share Value Col. 4	SAFE Col. 5	Cash Col. 6	Shares Bought (Sold) Col. 7	Shares Owned Col. 8	Port Control Col. 9	Buy (Sell) Advice Col. 10	Mrk Order (Sell) Buy Col. 11	6% Int Col 12	Comm	Port Value Col 13
10/94		11.00	6567	656	4088	-	597	6700	133	-	20	-	10,655
11/94		11.37	6791	679	4108	-	597	6700	(91)	-	20	-	10,899

Now November '94 and the stock has risen a little. Remember the beauty of the system: buy low and sell high. Watch it work. Okay, SHARE PRICE has risen to $11.37. Write it in SHARE PRICE and number of SHARES OWNED and PORTFOLIO CONTROL, which didn't change since no buying last month. Now multiply number of shares 597 X SHARE PRICE $11.37 and your SHARE VALUE is $6,791. Again SAFE is 10% of SHARE VALUE or 679. CASH has earned another $20 of INTEREST, write that in column 12 and add the $20 to CASH total in col. 6. Look at SHARE VALUE and PORTFOLIO CONTROL and as you thought, SHARE VALUE is higher which could possibly signal a sell. Write SHARE VALUE on top and PORTFOLIO CONTROL below as shown here:

SHARE VALUE	$6,791
- PORTFOLIO VALUE	6,700
= SELL ADVICE	$91

Now compare your (SELL) ADVICE to SAFE and you see that SAFE overrules any selling this month.

MARKET ORDER again is $0 but we use a – instead of writing $0. Again finish off the month by figuring your PORTFOLIO VALUE: SHARE VALUE + CASH or $6,791 + $4,108 = $10,899 or your investment is up $899. Keep thinking long-haul.

DECEMBER 1994

Date Col. 1	Remark Col. 2	Share Price Col. 3	Share Value Col. 4	SAFE Col. 5	Cash Col. 6	Shares Bought (Sold) Col. 7	Shares Owned Col. 8	Port Control Col. 9	Buy (Sell) Advice Col. 10	Mrk Order (Sell) Buy Col. 11	6% Int Col 12	Comm	Port Value Col 13
11/94		11.37	6791	679	4108	-	597	6700	(91)	-	20	-	10,899
12/94		11.75	7015	701	4128	-	597	6700	(315)	0	20	-	11,143

Now December '94. Again look up the SHARE PRICE (it's $11.75). Write it in column 3. Now go to column 8, SHARES OWNED and column 9, PORTFOLIO CONTROL; since you did nothing last month both stayed the same. Now continue business as usual.

Multiply the number of shares (597 X SHARE PRICE $11.75) and your SHARE VALUE is $7,015 write it in column 4. CASH was only affected by INTEREST so add $20 to this month's total and write $20 in column 12, INTEREST. Now compare PORTFOLIO CONTROL to SHARE VALUE. SHARE VALUE is $7,015 and bigger than PORTFOLIO CONTROL so you place it on top. Again

28

remember P for purchase if PORTFOLIO CONTROL is on top and S for sell if SHARE VALUE is on top. Very simple. So do your calculations:

SHARE VALUE	$7,015
- PORTFOLIO CONTROL	6,700
= (SELL) ADVICE	$315
- SAFE	701
= MARKET (SELL) ORDER	$ 0

You do nothing. Then you figure PORTFOLIO VALUE. Remember how? See this is easy. You added SHARE VALUE of $7,015 + CASH of $4,128 = $11,143. You're ahead $1,143.

Now we will skip some months. Every month you do the same process and calculations. Here is what things will look like in May 1995.

MAY 1995

Date Col. 1	Remarks Col. 2	Share Price Col. 3	Share Value Col. 4	SAFE Col. 5	Cash Col. 6	Shares Bought (Sold) Col. 7	Shares Owned Col. 8	Port Control Col. 9	Buy (Sell) Advice Col. 10	Mrk Order (Sell) Buy Col. 11	6% Int Col 12	Comm	Port Value Col 13
4/95		13.12	7009	700	5108	-	534	6700	(309)	0	25	-	12,117
5/95		13.87	7409	740	5134	+72 sh	534	6700	(709)	0	26	-	12,543

The SHARE PRICE is $13.87. Since you didn't buy or sell anything last month, SHARES OWNED AND PORTFOLIO CONTROL remained the same. SHARE VALUE is $7,409 (534 X $13.87), SAFE is 740. CASH was only affected by INTEREST, so add the $26 INTEREST earned ($5,108 X 1.005 = $5,134). Again check PORTFOLIO CONTROL and SHARE VALUE and again PORTFOLIO CONTROL is lower so PORTFOLIO CONTROL goes on the bottom:

SHARE VALUE	$7,409
- PORTFOLIO CONTROL	6,700
= (SELL) ADVICE	$709
- SAFE	740
= MARKET (SELL) ORDER	$ 0

All that's left to figure is PORTFOLIO VALUE ($7,409 + $5,134 = $12,543.)

Readjusting Cash/Stock Ratio

We are going to do an important step to increase our profits – readjust the cash/stock ratio. When we started out, we used 2/3 stock and 1/3 cash. Checking after one year, we find that the percentage of cash has increased. We want to take this excess cash and buy more stock with that. Our PORTFOLIO VALUE was $12,543. 1/3 of that is $4,139. Our current cash amount is $5,134 so: $5,134 - $4,139 = $995 of extra cash. We use that extra cash to buy the + 72 shares you will see in the June 1995 spreadsheet entry. That's why you see (709) in BUY (SELL) ADVICE but the actual BUY (SELL) ADVICE is BUY 995 in MARKET ORDER BUY. I wanted to show you what you will do in this case.

JUNE 1995

Date Col. 1	Remarks Col. 2	Share Price Col. 3	Share Value Col. 4	SAFE Col. 5	Cash Col. 6	Shares Bought (Sold) Col. 7	Shares Owned Col. 8	Port Control Col. 9	Buy (Sell) Advice Col. 10	Mrk Order (Sell) Buy Col. 11	6% Int Col 12	Comm	Port Value Col 13
5/95	Adjust s/c	13.87	7409	740	5134	+72 sh	534	6700	(709)	995	26	-	12,543
6/95		15.87	9620	962	4160	(61)	606	7695	(1925)	(963)	21	-	13,780

Onto June '95. The explanations are becoming shorter because you're getting smarter and seeing how easy this is. The SHARE PRICE rises to $15.87 a share. Write it down and then do columns 8 and 9. Column 8, SHARES OWNED, will increase by the 72 shares we bought last month with the excess cash (534 + 72 = 606). Column 9, PORTFOLIO CONTROL increases **BY 100% of the MARKET ORDER BUY amount of $995.** Whenever we first buy or add additional money to the system, we increase PORTFOLIO CONTROL by 100% – not the usual 50%. Thus column 9 is 6,700 + 995 = 7,695.

SHARE VALUE is 606 X $15.87 = $9,620. SAFE is always 10% of SHARE VALUE so SAFE is 962. CASH was affected by readjusting our stock/cash ratio. We started with $5,134 - $995 excess cash ׀ INTEREST of $21 = $4,160. PORTFOLIO CONTROL is again smaller:

SHARE VALUE	$9,620
- PORTFOLIO CONTROL	7,695
= (SELL) ADVICE	$1,925
- SAFE	962
= MARKET (SELL) ORDER	$963

You have a (SELL) MARKET ORDER. Divide $963 by the SHARE PRICE of $15.87 and you find that you sell (61) shares. Write in column 7. Then end the month by figuring your PORTFOLIO VALUE. $9,620 + $4,160 equals $13,780.

Let's skip ahead several months since you should see how easy this works. Again, in my complete book if you ask for it you will see all of these months in full detail. Let's jump ahead to April 1996.

April 1996

Date Col. 1	Remarks Col. 2	Share Price Col. 3	Share Value Col. 4	SAFE Col. 5	Cash Col. 6	Shares Bought (Sold) Col. 7	Shares Owned Col. 8	Port Control Col. 9	Buy (Sell) Advice Col. 10	Mrk Order (Sell) Buy Col. 11	6% Int Col 12	Comm	Port Value Col 13
3/96		16.12	6692	669	7918	21	415	7695	1003	334	39	-	14,610
4/96		18.12	7903	790	7622	-	436	7862	(41)	0	38	-	15,525

The SHARE PRICE is $18.12, up $2 from last month up. Go to columns 8 and 9. You bought 21 shares last month so your SHARES OWNED has increased from 415 to 436. PORTFOLIO CONTROL will increase since we did buy stock. Divide 334 by 2 and add that amount to PORTFOLIO CONTROL (334 divided by two = 167 + 7,695 equals 7,862). Write these two numbers in. SHARE VALUE is 436 X $18.12 equals $7,903. SAFE is 790. CASH is $7,918 - $334 + $30 INTEREST = $7,622. Again compare PORTFOLIO CONTROL and SHARE VALUE and SHARE VALUE is slightly higher. Do your calculations:

SHARE VALUE	$7,903
- PORTFOLIO CONTROL	7,862
= (SELL) ADVICE	$41
- SAFE	790
= DO NOTHING	$0

All that's left is to figure is PORTFOLIO VALUE. It's $7,903 + $7,622 = $15,525. So on this example that is a real stock, you would be ahead 55% for two years. Study this example and you'll see how you made your profit. The stock went steadily up for almost 2 years. Buy low and sell high shouldn't only be a cliché. It should and is put into practice through the system and produces the results you want from an investment.

OTHER SYSTEM MECHANICS WORTH KNOWING

Adding Additional Money

I didn't include an example of adding additional money to a stock. It is very easy. If you have for example an additional $1,000, you tell your broker to buy $500 worth of LEAPS and put $500 in your money market account (on a 50% LEAPS, 50% CASH type of investment). Then you increase PORTFOLIO CONTROL by the amount you bought LEAPS with ($500). Make a separate line on your spreadsheet to show the increase. Change all the columns that need changing. See the chart for Claire's Stores at the end of this Chapter for an example. Adding money is good to do for three reasons. It increases the size of your investment, decreases the relative cost of commissions, and increases your profits. As you read later, you should work toward 10 stocks, ETFs, closed-end funds with LEAPs to reduce risk. Also I recommend only adding money to an existing stock when the stock price is at or near its 52-week low.

SKIPPING A MONTH

In several charts in my free full-length book, you'll see dashes across one whole month except for INTEREST. For these months you skipped the system – it's not a rigid system you must do every month or whatever schedule you use to check on your investments with AIM. For these months the only thing that happened was earning INTEREST on your CASH. You only needed to write in the INTEREST earned that month and then you added and then next month you can add two months INTEREST the next month when you go back to the system.

STOCK SPLITS

Another thing I wanted to tell you. For stock splits, I figured the split after any of the transactions. For example, if you own 500 shares, sold 100 shares and then the stock split 3-for-2 then your calculations were: 500 – 100 = 400 X 1.5 = 600 shares now owned. You only need to change the SHARES OWNED column. I have included a blank spreadsheet you can copy to use at the end of the PDF version of my book that you will receive for free after buying this e-book version.

READJUSTING THE CASH/STOCK RATIO

One last item. At least once a year, readjust the stock/cash ratio to whatever ratio you are using for your particular type of investment. Different types of investments could have a different ratio between CASH and STOCK. I didn't do that in this chapter except once to keep the example simple. It's easy. Once a year I adjusted the stock/cash ratio back to 1/3 cash and 2/3 stock.

If the CASH balance was higher than 1/3 of the PORTFOLIO CONTROL, I took the excess CASH and bought more shares, and increased PORTFOLIO CONTROL by **100%** of the CASH amount I used to buy more shares. Look at how I did it and you'll understand. Do this anytime you readjust the cash/stock ratio.

Remember when we are investing in long-term options (LEAPS) we start with 50% LEAPS/50% CASH. We need to adjust the Cash/LEAPS ratio back to 50%-50% when it gets out of balance – for ex. If LEAPS are worth $8,000 & Cash is worth $12,000 – then we want to get back to $10,000 LEAPS - $10,000 Cash. We take $2,000 from Cash and use it to buy more LEAPS contracts. Normally we can't get exactly 50%-50% but just get closer to 50-50 ratio by buying closest number of contracts you can.

At the end of Chapter 2 in the PDF free full-length version of my investing book, you will find a spreadsheet showing Claire's Stores for the entire two years and you will find a blank spreadsheet that you can you can use to set up a Word spreadsheet to do your investing online. Below I am also including the table for all two years of Clair's Stores and the blank spreadsheet here. Please email me if you would like the actual file that shows these results.

DATE Col.1	REMARK Claire's Col.2	SHARE PRICE Col. 3	SHARE VALUE Col. 4	SAFE Col.5	CASH Col.6	SHARES BOUGHT (SOLD) Col. 7	SHARES OWNED Col. 8	PORT CONTROL Col. 9	BUY (SELL) ADVICE Col. 10	MKT ORD (SELL) BUY Col. 11	6 % INT Col. 12	PORT VALUE Col. 13
6/94		10.25	6700	670	3300	·	654	6700	·	·	·	10,000
7/94		10.00	6540	654	3317	·	654	6700	160	0	17	9,857
8/94		12.37	8093	809	3334	(47)	654	6700	(1393)	(584)	17	11,427
9/94		12.50	7588	758	3938	(10)	607	6700	(888)	(130)	20	11,526
10/94		11.00	6567	656	4088	·	597	6700	133	0	20	10,655
11/94		11.37	6791	679	4108	·	597	6700	(91)	0	20	10,899
12/94		11.75	7015	701	4128	·	597	6700	(315)	0	20	11,143
1/95		11.62	6940	694	4148	·	597	6700	(240)	0	20	11,088
2/95		14.12	8433	843	4168	(63)	597	6700	(1733)	(890)	20	12,601
3/95		12.62	6742	674	5083	·	534	6700	(42)	0	25	11,825
4/95		13.12	7009	700	5108	·	534	6700	(309)	0	25	12,117
5/95		13.87	7409	740	5134	+ 72 sh	534	6700	(709)	buy 995	26	12,543
6/95	adjust s/c	15.87	9620	962	4160	(61)	606	7695	(1925)	(963)	21	13,780
7/95		18.12	9878	987	5149	(66)	545	7695	(2183)	(1196)	26	15,027
8/95		19.50	9341	934	6377	(37)	479	7695	(1646)	(712)	32	15,718
9/95		20.75	9172	917	7124	(27)	442	7695	(1477)	(560)	35	16,296
10/95		20.50	8508	850	7722	·	415	7695	(813)	0	39	16,231
11/95		19.50	8093	809	7762	·	415	7695	(398)	0	39	15,855
12/95		18.62	7729	772	7801	·	415	7695	(34)	0	39	15,530
1/96		17.62	7314	731	7840	·	415	7695	381	0	39	15,154
2/96		19.00	7885	788	7879	·	415	7695	(190)	0	39	15,764
3/96		16.12	6692	669	7918	21	415	7695	1003	334	39	14,610
4/96		18.12	7903	790	7622	·	436	7862	(41)	0	38	15,525
4/96	Add'l $1000				+ 330			add 670		670		
5/96	·	·	·	·	·	·	·	·	·	·	38	·

DATE	REMARK	SHARE PRICE	SHARE VALUE	SAFE	CASH	SHARES BOUGHT (SOLD)	SHARES OWNED	PORT CONTROL	BUY (SELL) ADVICE	MKT ORD (SELL) BUY	6 % INT	COMM AMT	PORT VALUE

CHAPTER 5

How to Use LEAPS in a Severe Bear Market

It's now the end of January 2008. The stock market has had a pretty severe bear market for the past half a year or more. And this bear market has severely affected our model LEAPS portfolio. I have found that LEAPS react quite severely in a bear market. Also LEAPS react quite strongly when a stock becomes a bear that isn't going to recover. Based on actual real world experience, I am writing this chapter to see what we can do about severe bear markets that will improve the performance of our LEAPS. Also what can we do to prevent ourselves from being stuck with the investment that offers little or no hope of a recovery? I will start off by showing you two examples of what we want to prevent. Below are the spreadsheets again in the PDF free version showing how Advanced Micro Devices (AMD) and Starbucks have done in the current Bear Market.

DATE	REMARK AMD Jan 09 S 30	SHARE PRICE	SHARE VALUE	SAFE	CASH	Contracts BOUGHT (SOLD)	SHARES OWNED	PORT CONTROL	BUY (SELL) ADVICE	MKT ORD (SELL) BUY	Int.	# of Conts	PORT VALUE
11/06		3.45	11734	1173	5867	-	3400	11734	-	-	28	34	17,601
12/06		3.10	10540	1054	5839	-	3400	11734	1194	-		34	16,379
12/06		2.95	10030	1003	5658	-	3400	11754	1704	Lng 701	(29)	34	15,898
12/06	Buy at 2.67	2.70	9180	918	3668	6	3400	11734	2554	1602	15	40	15,048
12/06		3.20	12800	1280	4231	-	4000	12535	(265)	-	-	40	17,031
1/07		2.65	10600	1060	4231	3	4000	12535	1935	795	15	43	14,851
1/07		2.03	8729	872	4231	19	4300	12535	3806	3887	25	62	12,980
1/07		.96	12152	1215	371	7	6200	14340	2188	1372	16	69	12,523
1/07		1.77	12263	1226	(1001)	8	6900	15026	2761	1416	14	78	11,264
1/07		1.25	9750	975	(2431)	40	7800	15729	5979	5000	38	118	7,319
2/07		1.15	13570	1357	(7469)	29	11800	18229	4659	3306	29	147	6,101
2/07		1.13	16611	1611	(7469)	11	14700	19882	3271	1243	13	158	5807
2/07		1.08	17064	1706	(12060)	21	15800	20504	3440	2268	24	179	5,004
2/07		1.09	19511	1951	(14332)	-	17900	21638	2127	196	-	179	5,139
2/07		1.00	17900	1790	(14352)	19	17900	21638	3738	1900	22	198	3,548
3/07	30%s - 4989	.84	16632	1663	(16274)	12	19800	22588	5936	1008	17	210	358
3/07	BI 1.64	.78	16380	1638	(17299)	-	21000	23092	6712	-	-	-	(919)
3/09	30%S - 4914	.79	16590	1659	(17299)	23	21000	23092	6502	1817	25	233	(709)
3/07	30S - 5241	.73	17009	1700	(19141)	17	23300	24001	6992	1241	21	250	(1,666)
3/07	40%S - 6800	.65	16250	1625	(20404)	29	25000	24622	8372	1885	30	279	(4,154)
3/07	MKT - 50					30 con							
3/07		.55	15345	1534	(22319)	-	27900	25565	10220	Lgn 8686	-	279	(6,974)
3/07	Order 30@ 50	.50	13950	13950	(22319)	30	27900	25565	11613	1500	30	309	(8,369)
4/07		.55	16993	1699	(23830)	-	30900	26315	9320	-	-	309	(6,855)
5/07	70%s - 10164	.47	14523	1452	(23830)	30	30900	26315	11792	1410	31	339	(9,327)
5/07		.40	13560	1356	(25291)	-	33900	27020	-	-	-	-	(11,731)
5/07		.45	15255	1525	(25291)	-	33900	27020	-	-	-	-	(10,036)
6/07		.35	11865	1186	(25291)	30	33900	27020	15155	1050	31	369	(13,426)
6/07	110%S 13046	.32	11808	1180	(26372)	69	36900	27545	15737	2208	60	438	(14,564)
6/07		.29	12702	1270	(28640)	-	28649	28649	-	-	-	-	(15,938)
7/07	85%S - 13031	.35	15330	1533	(28640)	-	43800	28649	13319	Lgn 288	-	438	(13,310)
7/05	45%S - 8870	.45	19710	1971	(28640)	-	43800	28649	8939	Lgn 69	-	438	(8,930)
9/07		.30	13140	1314	(28640)	-	43800	28649	13509	-	-	438	(15,500)
10/07		.27	11826	1182	(28640)	-	43800	28649	-	-	-	438	(16,814)
11/07		.23	10074	1007	(28640)	-	43800	28649	-	-	-	438	(18,566)
11/07		.27	11826	1182	(28640)	(50)	43800	28649	16823	(1350)	46	388	(16,814)
11/07		.18	6984	698	(27336)	(100)	38800	28649	21665	(1800)	83	288	(20,352)
12/07		.14	4032	403	(25619)	(150)	28800	28649	24617	(2100)	105	134	(21,587)
12/07	Sold all	.13	1742	174	(23629)	(134)	13400	28649	26907	(1742)	86	0	(21,973)

You can see that AMD was a big loser. Now we want to prevent ourselves from getting hurt by future bad picks. How can we do that? The first thing to think about is should we have bought AMD in the first place?

Now we know we can make great profits buying LEAPS on safe Dow Jones stocks – I recommend as a beginner you stick with Dow Jones stocks' LEAPS – later on when you are an experienced AIM investor you can consider LEAPS on other stocks.

Frankly I thought AMD was a good buy when bought. It was down and to me prospects for the future looked good. Investors with "deep pockets" could have made high profits if they had held onto AMD LEAPS. It would have made them multi-millionaires over the past

30 years. Rolling over the LEAPs to longer-term LEAPs would have made them a ton of money. Again, be patient and in this for the long haul. Always remember short-term "paper losses" will equal long term "real profits."

But since I am editing this several years later if we had the courage to help hang onto the AMD LEAPs and use the Bear Strategy we would've made a ton of money. Like I told you earlier; go to Yahoo Finance and do historical prices on AMD say from January 2008 to the present and see how much up-and-down action you got and the stock didn't gain or lose nearly as much as the LEAP did.

That's why if you're only buying a few LEAPs, stick to the "blue chip" LEAPs like the ones I now feature in my newsletter. Again, we all know what level of risk we can handle and if you can handle a LEAP like AMD going up and down like it did you will make a great deal of money if you are patient. And the same thing happened with Crocs; a unique type of Shoe Company that went all the way down from $22 to $1 and then went back up into the $30s. See 5 years of CROC up and down in the last chapter of my full-length book.

In reviewing how I handled AMD I find I wasn't aggressive enough in waiting to buy when the price of the LEAP went down. I just wasn't aware that LEAPs could sink so far in a Bear market. In the future when you own a LEAP, you must really analyze when to buy and how much to buy. In the future I will take a much stronger stance and will wait to buy initially in the down market. A good rule of thumb would be to wait until your LEAP drops 50% before making your first buy. So for example if you bought a LEAP that was $4 a share or $400 a contract then you wait until the LEAP drops to $2 a LEAP or $200 a contract and then you make your first buy. And also use an aggressive bear SAFE to make a minimum buy of around $1,000 worth of new LEAP shares or even less.

You'll see looking at AMD that it was originally bought at $3.45 a share. This was a low price at the time comparing the LEAPs high/low history. But as hindsight shows, we bought new shares too soon. The first buy was made at $2.70 and following the history of AMD, you will see many other buys were made too soon. Since AMD was a risky LEAP, I should've waited until it dropped the 50% before making the first buy or set up an automated sell order at say 50% of the initial price. You can see that by not doing that we set ourselves up for a big loss that has very little chance of ever being recovered in the short term but a great chance to be recovered over the long-term.

Based on my experiences with AMD and other non-Dow Jones LEAPS I decided that you should limit yourself to "blue chip" LEAPs (like the Dogs of the Dow in the last chapter and monthly in my newsletter) initially or really understand how volatile a non-blue-chip could be before you purchase it as an initial LEAP in your portfolio and be able to handle the emotional and financial risks. Even if you buy a conservative LEAP, that doesn't mean you will eliminate the risk entirely. The nature of the beast is that a LEAP will always be a lot more volatile than the stock it derives its value from. Even on very conservative stocks, LEAPs can fall sharply. Take a look at Citigroup.

As you can see (in the upcoming table) Citigroup has fallen quite sharply but not as bad as AMD. Citigroup shows no signs of ever recovering even close to what it originally was). I always think they will rise but that is not always true.

DATE	REMARKS Citigroup Jan 10 S 45	SHARE PRICE	SHARE VALUE	SAFE	CASH	Contracts BOUGHT (SOLD)	SHARES OWNED	PORT CONTROL	BUY (SELL) ADVICE	MKT ORD (SELL) BUY	6% Int	Con Owned	PORT VALUE
9/07		7.68	15360	1536	7589		2000	15360	-	-	20	20	22,949
10/07		6.75	13500	1350	7625		2000	15360	-	-	(38)	20	21,125
10/07		6.45	12900	1290	7625	2	2000	15360	2460	1290	10	22	20,525
10/07		5.80	12760	1276	6325	2	2200	16005	3245	1160	10	24	19,085
11/07	20% S 2568	5.45	13080	1308	5155	2	2400	16585	3505	1090	10	26	18,235
11/07	30%S 3666	4.70	12220	1222	4055	2	2600	17130	4910	940	10	28	16,275
11/07	35% 4312	4.20	11760	1176	3105	2	2800	17600	5280	840	10	30	14,865
11/07	40%S 4960	4.20	12600	1260	2255	3	3000	18020	5420	1260	10	33	14,855
11/07		4.10	13530	1353	1623	-	3300	18650	-	-	(8)	33	15,153
11/07	60%S 6432	3.40	11220	1122	1623	3	3300	18650	7430	1020	10	36	12,843
12/07	75%S 7830	2.90	10440	1044	593	4	3600	19160	8720	1160	11	40	11,033
12/07		2.55	10200	1020	(578)	-	4000	19740	-	-	-	40	9,622
12/07		2.26	9040	904	(578)	-	4000	19740	-	-	-	40	8,462

I strongly advise beginning investors to stick to Dow Jones LEAPS because they will make you high profits and are very safe.

Remember my cardinal rule for investing – buy at or near the 52-week low. But even with that strategy, you can't guarantee that you will buy at the absolute bottom. So even with the "conservative" LEAPs, you run the chance of a sharp drop before the LEAP recovers. Again be cautious on when to make the buys and be cautious on how much you buy. When you see that 75% S above in the REMARKS column, it means that instead of a 10% SAFE (or 10% of the SHARE VALUE) I used a 75% S (or I used 7.5 times the amount of the 10% SAFE or I used 75% of the SHARE VALUE price for the SAFE amount.

Thus in the example above which you'll find somewhere in that spreadsheet; PORTFOLIO CONTROL $19,160 – SHARE VALUE $10,440 = $8,720 - 75% SAFE $7,830 = about $1,000 worth of new LEAPs to buy. Thus I only bought $1,160 worth of new LEAPs at $2.90 a LEAP or bought 4 more contracts. I wanted to be very cautious in case Citigroup went down further. As you can see from the spreadsheet Citigroup did go down further. But I feel a small buy at $2.90 was still warranted because we don't know what the bottom will be and $2.90 to me is still a good price to buy some more Citigroup LEAPs at.

Let's be conservative in the future and always go 50% CASH and 50% LEAPs instead of 2/3 LEAPs and 1/3 CASH. It will be better to have that extra cash to make buys with.

So let's summarize the advice I'm giving you for LEAPs in bear markets:

1. Analyze the parent stock very closely before buying the LEAP. Have a look at historical prices in Yahoo Finance. Stick with more conservative, blue-chip stocks (Dow Jones stocks) in the beginning until you get experienced with LEAPS. They can still be risky but will offer greater upside potentials when the market goes back to the bull.

2. Don't make the first buy until the LEAP price has dropped enough to buy the number of contracts you want (good rule of thumb – if you own 10 contracts wait till the LEAPS price drops enough to buy 3 contracts. Make future buys using high bear SAFE amounts like I talked about above. Try to keep your actual buys around $1,000 saving your CASH for future buys if the LEAP goes lower.

3. Start with 50% CASH, 50% LEAP ratio. Better to be more conservative and have more CASH for buys.

4. Ignore small changes both up and down. When we buy a LEAP in a bear market, we are expecting a big decrease sometime in the two years until the LEAP expires. Thus we don't want to buy or sell too quickly but rather get more LEAPs as cheaply as possible and sell those LEAPs for good profits when the parent stock recovers from whatever it

drove down. We must be patient.

5. It's best to start with say 10 different LEAPs (meaning LEAPS on 10 different stocks) if you're a big risk taker type of investor so we can have a variety. But in a bear market, most if not all of your LEAPs could go down from your initial purchase price even though you bought them thinking all the bad news was out. Look at how Citibank sank after its initial bad news. It still had more bad news and the market reacted to that bad news and drove the stock and LEAP even lower. That's why the 50% initial CASH is a good idea – use that extra cash and maximize our bear strategy for buys which will leave us with the best chance of maximizing our cash to make cheap buys. Remember at some point the stock and LEAP will start going up and staying up. But not for all stocks and LEAPs.

6. Here's another trick I learned since I originally wrote this book. Remember how I said that LEAPs will expire in January of any given year. But really any LEAP you own never has to expire because you can always roll it over to the LEAP in the following year so for example if you own a January 2017 LEAP, you can always roll it over to a January 2018 LEAP and buy an extra year of time.

7. Another great idea as I edit this. You are not limited to only buying call LEAPs (make money when stock goes up). You can also buy put LEAPs (make money when stock goes down.)

This is not the perfect answer to LEAPs in a severe bear market but it offers you good ideas to increase profits with LEAPs in a bear market. If you have any other good ideas for improving this chapter I'd love to hear them. E-mail your ideas to me at jeff@jjjinvesting.biz.

CHAPTER 6

The Right Ratio for LEAPS and Cash

Robert Lichello, the inventor of the AIM system, originally came out with the idea of using 50% cash and 50% shares when you start an AIM investment. So for example if you're investing $10,000 into a stock you would start with $5,000 worth of cash and $5,000 worth of stock. But then Mr. Lichello changed his recommendation to having 2/3 stock & 1/3 Cash.

I went along with the 2/3 stock/1/3 cash split for many years until I finally encountered a severe bear market around the year 2000. When you have a severe bear market your cash ratio can go down substantially. And if you look in my book, and look at how Campbell Resources did for 3 years you will see that you might need very deep pockets to come up with additional cash that AIM calls for if you started with the 2/3, 1/3 arrangement and also you are using the 10% SAFE amount to determine buys and sells.

Since I have been playing with AIM for many years I have done considerable thinking on good ways to tweak the game to help you make maximum profits. And one way you can make additional profits is by the wise use of the ratio of shares and cash.

Different kinds of investments call for different kinds of ratios between the share amount and the cash amount. I'll give you some examples below so that you have a better idea of what I am talking about.

CLOSED-END FUND

A closed-end fund is a special type of mutual fund. The biggest difference between a closed-end fund and a regular mutual fund is the fact that a regular mutual fund can constantly add money to the fund as new investors put money into the fund. For example Fidelity Magellan many years ago was considered one of the top mutual funds in the United States. It grew and grew from a small amount to I believe over $5 billion. Basically all mutual funds are open which means they can continue to grow as new investors put money in. But also they can shrink if mutual fund investors start taking their money out of the fund.

I have never liked regular mutual funds to use for AIM investing because of many restrictions on buying and selling and many fees and I always felt that closed-end investments were a better way to use AIM than open mutual funds were.

Here's a quick way to explain what a closed-end fund is. Somebody decides on an objective for a closed-end fund. For example, they could represent all the good companies in Brazil, China, or it could be designed to bring in high levels of dividends – there are many different objectives you'll find with a closed-end fund.

The nice thing about closed-end funds is this. And I would use as an example one that I have recommended in the past and still recommend called AGNC. Let me explain how the mutual fund is set up and works and why it is good for AIM investing.

When a fund like AGNC is set up, they issue let's say for example 10 million shares at $10 each. The shares are issued just like shares in a stock. So, these 10 million shares are bought by investors. The closed-end fund gets listed on one of the stock exchanges, normally the New York Stock Exchange. Once the 10 million shares are sold, the only way for a new investor to buy shares in that closed-end fund is to buy shares on a stock exchange from somebody who owns the shares. Basically just the same way you would buy shares of stock you traded on the stock market and you buy somebody else's sells.

The advantage is now that a closed-end fund trades on the stock exchange you can buy and sell instantly you don't have to wait for the end of the day and for the net asset value to be determined. Also closed-end funds are much more likely to have better highs and lows than regular mutual funds. And closed-end funds are just as conservative as an open mutual fund but without any of the drawbacks.

Another example is HYF that closed in June 2016. This is an example of a great closed-end fund for investors that are looking for a monthly dividend and a high monthly dividend to boot and also a little up-and-down action using AIM at the same time. This fund is at a very low price and in the last year the high was around $2.66 and the low was $1.83. And HYF paid a dividend of a little over 10% a year. (This in the 2008 timeframe; HYF close in June 2016.)

For about the first 10 years I was using AIM; I always recommended blindly using two thirds shares and one third for cash. But that was before the great bear market of 2000, 2001, and 2002. Then I worked on developing bear strategies to help investors conserve their cash when the market was in a severe bear turn and everything was going down.

The first thing I did was to return to Robert Lichello's original concept of 50% cash and 50% stock. But as you will see in Chapter 2 of this book, just using the 50% cash and share ratio will not prevent the depletion of your cash when your investment has a

48

severe bear turn. But if you have deep pockets the best system to use is the 50% cash 50% stock ratio and I'll explain it to you quickly.

Campbell Resources started off around $6.40 and about two years later was selling for $.85. Naturally AIM was gobbling up lots of cheap shares as Campbell Resources went down and down. For that example I used the mythical starting $10,000 that was split into $5,000 CASH and $5,000 SHARE VALUE.

When you look at the spreadsheets in Chapter 12 of my full-length free book you will see that you had to put in an additional $25,000 worth of cash to make all of the buys that AIM told you to make as Campbell Resources went down and down. There was a three month stretch when Campbell Resources was selling below $1.00 and AIM just gobbled up lots of cheap shares buying over 1,000 shares in each of those three months at extremely cheap prices.

But faithfully following AIM with the 10% buy amount and the 10% sell amount that Robert Lichello recommended, you eventually finished with a profit of 38% despite the fact that Campbell Resources finished down 62% after the three years.

So putting in all that additional money did pay off in the long run but not everybody has deep pockets and can put in additional cash when AIM calls for it. I realized that so I said I have to guide my AIM strategy to be more conservative and try and save cash as an investment goes steadily down.

As I was talking to my investor, it suddenly occurred to me that we could use different ratios depending on the different types of investments that he owns. He is invested into 3 LEAPs (a long-term option investment that expires in January of every given year, so for example now you have LEAPs that expire in January 2018 and January 2019.) He owns the one closed-end fund HYF and another

ETF or electronically traded fund with the symbol BOE. He also owns a very aggressive ETF from Direxion called the China Bull (YINN) (3X) leveraged that follows the Chinese market. This fund is leveraged so if the Chinese stock market or the Dow Jones Industrial Average for example goes up 3%, this fund with the symbol YINN would go up 9%.

When I talked to him yesterday he got me thinking about the ratios between cash and stock or shares and I decided to tell him that with the conservative closed-end fund HYF he did not really need to have a 50% cash and 50% share ratio. Like I said earlier he's owned HYF since August 2011 and since August 2011 his CASH account on that closed-end fund has gone from $9,400 down to $9,034 because we bought the 200 shares in October at the 52 week low of $1.83.

I told him right on the phone that HYF is a great dividend payer and the $9,000 in the CASH account with his broker in the money market is paying virtually 0% interest. I told him we could be more aggressive owning shares in HYF and right off the top of my head I recommended on Monday he buy another 1,000 shares at the market price of $2.16. He just doesn't need to have $9,000 worth of cash sitting with his broker earning no interest when this investment is very conservative, HYF will never need a very large amount of cash to make additional buys in the future. It's just a different kind of investment so now I'm going to be more aggressive on conservative investments and recommend to my investors that they put more money into shares and less money into cash.

He has another closed-end fund with the symbol BOE and I'm also going to check that one out and recommend to him that he put more money into shares and less money into cash.

STOCKS

Stocks are mixed bag. There are some stocks that are very conservative and then there are some stocks that can have pretty wild swings. In my original book *I Guarantee You Will Buy Low Sell High and Make Money*, I identified the two types of stocks - conservative stocks and semi-aggressive stocks. Conservative stocks to me are more like the traditional 30 stocks you find in the Dow Jones Industrial Average, stocks that have big names that are basically household words like AT&T, IBM, Boeing, General Electric, American Express, etc.

Semi-aggressive stocks on the other hand have wilder high/low swings; you can find stocks that might have a low of $3 and a high of $30. You would want to keep a 50-50 ratio for stocks that do have wild swings but you really could decrease the amount of cash in stocks that are conservative. I can't really make a blanket statement on any stock but from now on with my investors I will definitely advise them that I think you could have less cash sitting in your broker's money market account because of the type of stock or closed-end fund or ETF that you own.

LEAPS

LEAPS, like I said earlier, are long-term options on either a stock or ETF. Even LEAPS on very conservative stocks such as American Express, General Electric, IBM, can be extremely volatile. I would always recommend a blanket rule to keep 50% CASH and 50% LEAPS anytime you buy LEAPS. I even have a basic rule that you'll see in my other book that I don't even consider buying more LEAPS for one of my clients until the LEAPS has gone down at least 50%. That means for example if we bought a LEAP at $4 or $400 for one contract (you have to buy contracts with LEAPs which have 100 options; you cannot just buy 25 LEAPS) then I would wait until the LEAP went from $4 to $2 and then I would advise my client we should buy some more contracts.

The 50% can be modified if you decide to pick a higher price where AIM says sell a certain number of contracts or pick a lower price where AIM says buy a certain number of contracts. Good rule of thumb – if you own 10 contracts figure the higher price at which you would sell 3 contracts with AIM and figure the lower price where AIM tells you to buy 3 more contracts.

I think LEAPS should be in everybody's portfolio because they pay a much higher rate over the long term than the stock or ETF that they follow. LEAPS are as safe as the stock or ETF that you buy them on. And you can always sell (roll over) long term options (LEAPS) when they have one year of time remaining and buy new long-term options that have two years remaining before they expire. People think options are an expiring investment but by rolling over options you extend the expiration indefinitely.

ETF's

ETF's are a recent invention and have really only been around for about the last couple years. I think they are a great new invention to the world of investing. ETFs have all the advantages that closed-end funds have which means they trade on the stock market and you can instantly buy and sell them and they give you an expanded range into many different types of investments. And to compound the felony, you can even get LEAPs on some ETF's. I'll talk about that in another chapter.

With most ETF's I do not feel you need to have 50% cash and 50% ETF ratio when you initially start with the investment. Any investment that is a combination of other investments is always going to be safer than if you buy one stock or one LEAP. It's just the nature of the beast that something that is a collection of things can never be affected greatly by anyone of the multiple investments that is in the fund or the ETF. Also both closed-end funds and ETF's have management that went into the creation of and sometimes the continuing evolution of the ETF into the future. So you are actually getting a little bit of management when you own an ETF or a closed-end fund. So you can afford to be more aggressive owning shares in the fund or the ETF and have less CASH on your spreadsheet for that particular investment.

I want to emphasize that one size does not fit all when it comes to investing and that's why I think it helps you to have somebody like me advising you on how much CASH and how many shares should be in the ratio for any particular investment that you thinking of owning.

Some investors are very conservative, some investors want some income, some investors want to go for larger returns; maybe they're older in life and they don't have a lot of time to sit there and wait 20-30 years for their investments to make them lots of money and that's fine. AIM can handle any type of investor from the most conservative to the most risky. And again AIM will faithfully tell you exactly how much to buy, how much to sell, or to do nothing.

And the other beauty of AIM is that you can decide to have me supervise it for you. That means you will have me looking at your investments on a daily basis and notifying you whether to sell, whether to buy, or whether to do nothing. It's always better to actively manage investments than just buy them and forget them.

So I hope this helped you decide and give you a little information at least on the questions to ask when you start investing in AIM about how to maximize your profits with the minimal risk.

CHAPTER 7

Dogs of the Dow LEAPS for Investors

Dogs of the Dow LEAPS make the best profits on very safe investments – the Dow Jones Industrial Average 30 stocks. The Dogs are the 10 Dow Jones Average stocks that pay the highest dividends.

As you see in the Chapter 3 - How I'm Doing; only checking the price once a month from January 2014 to now (November 2016) would have made you 134% profits in the last 35 months. That's an average of about 50% a year!

And you're only spending 2 hours once a month checking the prices of the LEAPS. Checking once a month is even better than checking daily because you will get bigger high/low swings when you buy and sell which will make you higher long-term profits.

I give away a lot for free but would like to make some money for my 30 years+ of expertise. So if I have convinced you that this is a great lifetime way to make profits, have a great retirement, do the things you want in life and control your life yourself instead of having other people decide your life then hire me to help you set up the perfect portfolio for you and help you manage it until you feel comfortable doing AIM yourself. Most people find it best to have my help for 3 or 6 months at a time. My flat fee is a wise and small investment to gain a great way to invest for the rest of your life. You can contact me at jeff@jjjinvesting.biz

AIM (Automatic Investment Management) is a lot like backgammon

– you can learn to play in an hour or two but spend the rest of your life improving your play. I hope to inspire a passion for AIM investing in you that grows more intense as the years go by. And I want you to fulfill all your dreams.

To hire me to help you get started using AIM please email Jeff at jeff@jjjinvesting.biz and for a very low cost you can get started. I can't guarantee you future profits but I can tell you the Dow Jones stocks – not LEAPS – portfolio has grown 839% in the last 23 years which includes several very bearish periods like the Dot.com crash in 2000 & the housing market collapse in 2008. I can honestly say there has never been a losing trade with AIM because you only buy when prices are down and only sell when prices are up enough to be profitable.

I have enjoyed writing this revision and look forward to help you make your AIM profits.

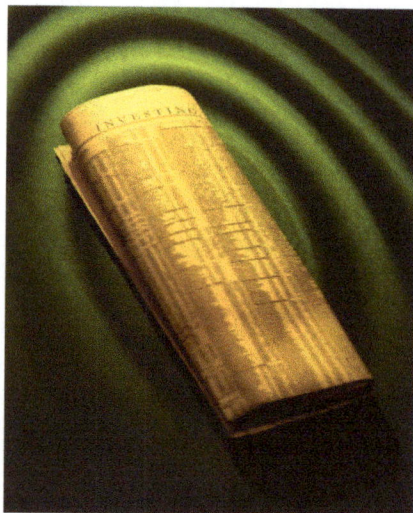

BONUS – MY SPECIAL TIPS & INSIGHTS

As I've worked on this book I have thought of some ideas and others have given me good ideas I'd like to share. Some of these ideas that may have mentioned already but it won't hurt repeating them.

Here's the best way to play the system:

1. Buy your stock initially when it is at or near its 52-week low.
2. Start looking up the prices of your stocks a few days before it's time to buy or sell.

If one or more of your stocks shows strong price changes, then postpone your buy or sell decision and follow the stock closely. I will give you an example: I owned Cray Computer and the day I was about to see if I should buy or sell, Cray went up $2 a share from $8.00 to $10.00. I waited a day; Cray went from $10.00 to $11.50. I waited another day; it went from $11.50 to $13.00. I waited another day, it went down $.50 a share and I sold based on the system. You can play this game too. If your stock is sharply going up or down, follow it day to day and get the maximum move before you buy or sell.

3. Here's the key to increased profits. Play your stock the regular way until it hits its 52–week high (the high should be at least 150% higher than your original purchase price). If you originally bought your stock at $5 a share, then $12.50 is 150% higher. When the stock hits the 52-week high, sell all the remaining shares and use the money to buy another stock at its 52-week low and repeat the process. You can always buy the same stock back when it's back at its 52-week low.

I envision you should have enough money to buy at least $1,000 worth of a new stock with the money you get from selling all remaining shares. Don't worry if you find out you now own $1,180 worth of your new stock. You can set up your new spreadsheet the same as you have in the past. Cash is now 1/2 of $1,180 or $590, which remember is, also 1/3 of your PORTFOLIO TOTAL, if this is a conservative stock – otherwise use 50% CASH – 50% shares.

4. Again, readjust your cash/stock ratio at least once a year. More often would be better. Check your ratio after you have a large sale. Remember you make your money buying and selling stock, not earning interest on your money market account with your broker. And in the days of 2016, your stockbroker is paying a mighty low percent of interest probably 1% or less.

5. Keep some of your regular savings money in your money market account that you converted to a high-paying Closed-End High Yield Fund paying 6-8% a year and has monthly dividends. You will make slightly higher interest on your money and you have a little extra cushion in case the system needs a little extra money to make some especially good buys at low prices. We're playing it close to the vest keeping our cash at 1/3 of our PORTFOLIO TOTAL and run the possibility of running out of cash occasionally just when the system is giving us great buys. Having that extra cash there will give you peace of mind. Now you can lend yourself money and you'll be playing the system the way you should. You'll quickly pay back that loan with your profits.

6. Always use "Buy to Open" when you buy LEAPS contracts and always use "Sell to Close" when you sell LEAPS contracts. NEVER USE "Buy to Close" or "Sell to Open"!!

7. Always use a "Limit" price for your initial buy & always use a price 10 or 15 cents lower than the last closing price the previous day. For example the LEAPS close at $3.00 or $300 a contract. Use a limit price of $2.90 or $2.85 and make sure you use the GTC (Good Till Canceled) button not the same day button. GTC keeps your order open for the next 3 months. But when you sell always use a "market" price to lock in profits immediately.

I hope this bonus section also showed you that you too can figure out some ideas on your own that will increase your profits. If so, please share them with me and I'll add them to a revised version and give you credit. Good investing ahead and to all the best.

HOW TO CONTACT JEFFREY WEBER

This is such a good way to invest you want to make sure you get started correctly – with the right long-term options (LEAPS) on the right Dow Jones stock for your particular investing situation. And you to do the AIM system correctly - anything new even if simple has a learning curve – use my 30 years' of experience to get started right on the road to lifetime profits. Contact me at jeff@jjjinvesting.biz to hire me to help you get started. You will be very happy with your results!

Thank you for buying my book – now let's get started making you great profits for life!!!